Basilici ganofolari.

Al. natur. c. i. z̃. f. i. f. melt creo. oxonferum. Juuamenti.
substancia ſtringit ſuccis laxar. nocumētuz. obtenebrat insti-
irmono nocumenti. cū foleis poztilace.

A Medieval
Herbal

⤳ ❧ ⤳

Ruta.

CHRONICLE BOOKS

SAN FRANCISCO

First published in the United States by Chronicle Books.

Copyright ©1994 by Pavilion Books, Ltd.

Jacket design: Laura Lovett
Calligraphy: Georgia Deaver
Printed in Singapore.

Library of Congress Cataloging-in-Publication Data
A Medieval herbal.
    72 p.   122 x 155mm
    ISBN 0-8118-0793-2
    1. Herbs—Therapeutic use. 2. Herbs—Utilization. 3. Herbs—
Folklore. 4. Medicine, Medieval. I. Chronicle Books (Firm)
    RM666.H33M443   1995
    615'.321—dc20
                                94-12340
                                CIP

Distributed in Canada by Raincoast Books,
112 East 3rd Avenue, Vancouver, B.C. V5T 1C8

10 9 8 7 6 5 4 3 2 1

Chronicle Books
275 Fifth St.
San Francisco, CA 94103

INTRODUCTION

THE GLIMPSES OF THE MEDIEVAL WORLD OFFERED BY extracts from early herbals reveal a universe quite different from our own. Herbals were books containing descriptions of the 'virtues' or properties of plants, together with collections of remedies and advice. They often included illustrations to help identify the subjects. Once you allow for artistic license in their portrayal, and translate the strange-sounding names, most of the plants become recognizable to modern eyes. But if the plants of the herbals seem familiar, the people using them and their preoccupations can seem worlds away.

Herbs were a solution or cure for an extraordinary mixture of diseases: we read of remedies for varieties of worms and warts, as well as stomach and head aches, heart and liver diseases. A need to treat states such as mental vacancy and 'idiotcy' is matched by more painful symptoms like 'sore of bladder'. There are occasional notes of caution: rue, prescribed as an anticoagulant, was not given to women in case it caused internal bleeding. Many herbs do possess antiseptic properties, but practices such as stuffing them into keyholes, strewing or burning them as fumigants, or wearing herb amulets were insufficient to ward off plague epidemics. Perhaps remedies were more successful on a psychological level, as when ladies gave knights a sprig of thyme to boost their courage. Simple measures to keep clean, such as a face-wash of daisies (picked at full moon) or strawberries for whitening the teeth, seem tame in comparison.

Herbs were the only drugs available in the Middle Ages. They were often dried – the name 'drug' possibly derives from the Anglo-Saxon *dregen*, meaning 'to dry'. Different parts of plants had different uses, whether for infusions, decoctions, ointments, or syrups; root, seed, and bark were used as well as flower and leaf. In addition to medicinal and culinary uses, herbs were made into dyes, inks, and incense. They were also widely used for cosmetics, perfumes, and toiletries, as they are today.

The medieval belief in the virtues of herbs meant that there was a living to be made by gathering the appropriate parts to sell in the marketplace or to apothecaries. Single herbs were known as 'simples', and from these drugs were compounded. Apothecaries and physicians also grew herbs in their own gardens. Climate, weather, habitat, soil, time of gathering and method of preserving all affect the properties of a plant. The medieval herbalist had to observe additional precautions: certain herbs 'must be picked at sunrise', while turning 'as the sun goes from east to south and west', and must be gathered 'without use of iron', often in silence, without looking behind one. Even more problematic was the mandrake, which was believed to scream when uprooted. To hear this shriek meant death. Having avoided this mishap by getting a dog to pull up the plant, you could use its mysterious powers against demoniacal possession or as a love potion, as well as to cure gout and sleeplessness.

Knowledge of plants and recipes for their use were passed on from generation to generation. A parallel repository of herb lore took the written form of the herbals, compiled and copied by the only people with clerical skills – the clerics themselves. As well as being the scribes and illuminators of the age, many were also influential early gardeners. Much of our knowledge of the part played by herbs in the medieval world is gleaned from the writings of the monks. Illustrations in the herbals were often copies of copies rather than accurate representations and plants appeared embellished with the myths surrounding them.

The earliest known herbal was written nearly five thousand years ago in China, by the emperor Shen Nung. The original does not survive, although it is known to have influenced many later herbals, fragments of which are still extant. The Sumerians and Egyptians recorded the use of herbs some two thousand years BC, the latter medicinally and for cosmetic and embalming ointments. Trade along the Mediterranean coast spread herbs and spices to Greece, where the famous doctor Hippocrates (born c. 460 BC) included some four hundred herbal remedies in his writings. His theories that disease was caused by an imbalance of the four bodily humours – the sanguine, phlegmatic, choleric, and melancholic, which reflected the four elements of earth, air, fire, and water and the attributes of being hot, cold, moist, or dry – were later developed by other Greek physicians. The theories remained influential well into the Middle Ages and the principle of treating the 'hot, dry' symptoms of a fever with an antidote of herbs that were 'cool and moist' was a basic tenet of medieval medicine.

The most important treatise on herbs was written in AD 1 by Dioscorides, a Greek physician working with the Roman army. *De Materia Medica* contains the names, descriptions, and virtues of six hundred plants. A 6th-century copy is the earliest surviving illustrated herbal, and its influence can be traced for over a thousand years.

As the Romans marched across and conquered Europe, they introduced many Mediterranean herbs and plants into more northerly latitudes. Some culinary herbs, such as fennel, ground elder, and alexanders, became naturalized and wild in Britain. Among other plants cultivated ever since are parsley, garlic, mint, thyme, hyssop, sage, dill, and savory. The Romans used lavender in their bath water (named after the Latin *lavare*, to wash) and soapwort for washing delicate fabrics.

During the Dark Ages after Rome fell, trade centred on Venice and the East, while northern Europe suffered from constant wars and invasions. Early records are scarce, so we have to rely on manuscripts and archaeological evidence to piece together the history of herbs. Monasteries and convents had to be self-sufficient

to survive, with an orchard, kitchen garden, and physic
garden planted with species of herbs in clumps for easy
identification. Caring for the sick was a Benedictine rule,
and it is from a 9th-century plan in the Benedictine
monastery of St Gallen in Switzerland that the most
detailed records survive of what was grown: sage,

horsemint, cumin, rue, lovage, fennel, fenugreek, mint, rosemary, kidney beans, and savory are familiar names from the list.

In ancient Britain, the Druid priest-healers of pre-Roman times studied astrology and combined the mystical with the practical in the use of medicinal herbs. In Wales, even before Hippocrates, medicine was important, and it is probable that knowledge of Greek theories spread through trade with Phoenicians. A 13th-century prince of South Wales had a physician, assisted by his three sons, at Myddfai, in Carmarthenshire. The family compiled a collection of medical recipes, including a list of one hundred and seventy-five plants and herbal preparations, in a document known as *The Physicians of Myddfai*.

Before the advent of printing and the acceptance of botany as a science, manuscript herbals were mainly the work of monks or compilations of earlier examples. Copies were made of southern European herbals, such as the *Herbarium* of Apuleius Platonicus, a Latin text which relied on Greek material, first compiled around AD 400. A famous early Anglo-Saxon herbal was the 10th-century *Leech Book of Bald*, which included prescriptions sent by the patriarch of Jerusalem to Alfred the Great. The text extracts that follow were mainly selected from these few early herbals.

Herbs and their uses were also discussed by authors of more general works. Bartholomaeus Anglicus, an English Franciscan who wrote the first encyclopedia in Latin, devoted a volume to herbs in his *De Proprietatibus Rerum* (on the properties of things) of 1240. The encyclopedic works of his German contemporary Albertus Magnus include a volume on plants, *De Vegetabilibus et Plantis*. An unknown author later published his version of the *Book of Secrets of Albertus Magnus*. Petrus Crescentiis, writing in Bologna in 1305, includes a volume on herbs in his horticultural and agricultural treatises *Liber Ruralium Commodorum*. He noted how good mint was for bad gums and recommended a mouth rinse of mint vinegar and the use of mint powder. He also talked of the importance of planting by the stars – much herb lore concerning sowing, harvesting, and gathering relates to the power of the elements, the forces of sun, moon, planets, and seasons.

The medical school at Salerno in southern Italy extended its influence in Europe from the 10th to the 13th centuries as crusaders returned north with respect for the medical care they had received there. Muslim physicians advanced the understanding of herbal properties. The medieval health handbooks, *Tacuinum Sanitatis*, were based on Arabic writings.

The advent of printing in the 15th century spread information about herbs, although manuscript herbals and copies continued to be produced for some years. Some of the best printed herbals were illustrated with woodcuts drawn from life. In mid-16th-century Germany, the herbals of Otto Brunfels, Jerome Bock and Leonhart Fuchs used woodcuts of finely observed detail, later much copied.

Fuchs' illustrations appeared in the *New Herball* by William Turner, published in three parts in 1551–68. Having travelled widely 'to knowe and se the herbes my selfe', Turner recorded some two hundred and thirty plants, and his approach marks the start of more systematic botanical study. Although Banckes' *Herball* of 1525 was the first to be printed in English, it was not until 1597 that a more popular gardening book was published, the *Herball or Generall Historie of Plantes* by John Gerard. Based on a translation of the Flemish botanist Rembert Dodoens' work, with Gerard's additional observations, it is included here (although scarcely medieval) for its importance as a bridge between the age of the herbal and a more modern approach to plant knowledge. From this point the ideas based on astrology, humours and the doctrine of signatures became outmoded, although they lingered on among ordinary folk who were ignorant of the results of advances in scientific inquiry.

The 'doctrine of signatures' according to the Swiss 16th-century physician Paracelsus, was a belief that each plant was 'signed' in some aspect of appearance, either in colour or shape, to indicate which illness it would cure. Thus, red clover (*Trifolium pratense*) might purify blood, or the red juice from St John's wort signified its power to heal wounds. *Hepatica nobilis*, with leaves resembling the liver, was used to cure hepatic diseases; lungwort (*Pulmonaria officinalis*), with leaves like the silvered surface of the lungs, to treat lung diseases, and the yellow marigold (*Calendula officinalis*) was used for jaundice.

Many active principles isolated from herbs are still in medical use today, including ones derived from cowslip, daisy, centaury, vervain, and betony; others have been synthesized chemically. In addition, herbs are used homoeopathically. Modern research has proved the age-old value of these herbs and has saved us from the trial and error associated with the recommendations of the medieval herbs.

However plausible these cures may have been in medieval times, it is to be stressed that their inclusion here is only for curiosity. Under no circumstances should they be attempted in practice, as some include poisonous plants.

OF A WOOD ...

WOODS BEN WIDE PLACES WAST AND DESOLATE Yᵗ many trees growe in wᵗoute fruyte and also few hauyinge fruyte. And those trees whyche ben bareyne and beereth noo manere fruyte alwaye ben generally more and hygher thãne yᵗ wyth fruyte, fewe out taken as Oke and Beche. In thyse wodes ben ofte wylde beestes and foulis. Therein growyth herbes, grasse, lees and pasture, and namely medycynall herbes in wodes foūde. In somer wodes ben bewtyed [beautied] wyth bowes and braunches, wᵗ herbes and grasse. In wode is place of disceyte [deceit] and of huntynge. For therin wylde beest ben hunted: and watches and disceytes [deceits] ben ordenyd and lette of houndes and of hunters. There is place of hidynge and of lurkyng.

BARTHOLOMAEUS ANGLICUS, *DE PROPRIETATIBUS RERUM*, 1240

BETONY

(Betonica officinalis)

A DRINK FOR A FIEND SICK MAN, TO BE DRUNK OUT OF A church bell; githrife, cynoglossum, yarrow, lupin, betony, attorlothe, cassock, flower de luce, fennel, church lichen, lichen, of Christs mark *or cross*, lovage; work up the drink off clear ale, sing seven masses over the worts, add garlic and holy water, and drip the drink into every drink which he will subsequently drink, and let him sing the psalm, Beati immaculati, and Exurgat, and Salvum me fac, deus, and then let him drink the drink out of a church bell, and let the mass priest after the drink sing this over him, Domine, sancte pater omnipotens. For a lunatic; costmary, goutweed, lupin, betony, attorlothe, cropleek, field gentian, hove, fennel; let masses be sung over, let it be wrought of foreign ale and of holy water; let him drink this drink for nine mornings, at every one fresh, and no other liquid that is thick and still, and let him give alms and earnestly pray God for his mercies.

LEECH BOOK OF BALD, Book 1, Chapter LXIII, 10th century

THESE ARE THE VIRTUES OF BETONY

H E WHO WILL HABITUATE HIMSELF TO DRINK THE JUICE, will escape the stranguary. If it is boiled in white wine, and drank, it will cure the colic, and swelling of the stomach. Pounding it small, expressing the juice and apply it with a feather to the eye of a man, will clear and strengthen his sight, and remove specks from his eye. The juice is a good thing to drop into the ears of those who are deaf.

The powder mixed with honey is useful for those who cough; it will remove the cough and benefit many diseases of the lungs. If boiled with leek seed, it will cure the eye, and brighten as well as strengthen the sight.

THE PHYSICIANS OF MYDDFAI, 13th century

BRAMBLE

(Rubus fruticosus)

1. FOR SORE OF EARS, TAKE THIS WORT, WHICH IS NAMED eruscus, and by another name bramble, so tender, pound it; then take the wash made lukewarm, drip it in the ear; it diminishes the sore, and surely healeth.

2. For flux of wife *(woman)*, take heads of this same wort, so tender, and of them let there be thrice seven; seethe in water to a third part; administer *(this)* to be drunk fasting for three days, so however, that thou every day renew the drink.

3. For heart ache, take leaves of this same wort, pounded by themselves; lay them over the left teat; the sore passes off.

4. For new wounds, take blossoms of this same wort, lay them to the wounds; without any delay and mischief, they will heal the wounds.

5. For sore of joints, take some part of this same wort, seethe in wine to the third part, and with the wine let then the joints be bathed; *(the application)* relieves all the infirmity of the joints.

THE HERBARIUM OF APULEIUS, 11th century

GRECIS DR

A lii
p rophete
A lii
A lii
J tali
R omani
A lii

Batosidea
Cinosbatos
Simrophu
Ematteanos
Emaudeos
Sinix
Rubum uocant
Rosa siluatica
DOLOREM
pressus mauriculi
dolore liberat

Nascetur in campis & insepibus.
Herbe crusci qui masculus &
f rupefactus & stillatus auriu
& psmart   dicimus.

D GRECA

Herba
ide. VIIII. mali
decoquant insc.
refrigid auert
pariciuni faciens miri
D PROFLUVIUM
qui mas teneras ter septinas

crusci qui mas umi. & mirte qui mas
quinati sicci cortices tires.
& catesinas myngue. & ciua
fomentabis tibi sessu. Hoc
sice stringit. & sanat.
AMULIERIS. Herbas rusci
decoquis maqua usq; ad

teras & triduo ieuno potu dab. ita.
ues potione.   D CARDIACOS. Herba crusci folia
imponuntur & mamillę sinistre dolore tollit. Ad vavs
CINGEBARU ET DOLORE VITA. Herbe crusei caules tenero...
muno decoquis & ipsu uinu more contnebis sume   factu.
vve REMEDIO. herbe crusci folia aresiam   insibni
inclauo facto. resilit inpresente nebo. Ad   VVLNERA RE CURIA
herbe crusci flos aut maros sine collecti   ones apiculo   sanat Ad enolo
mata. Herba rubii muno decocta   adeturas coq.   uino fouebis ...
lomquu & consia uina sedat. Nom SERPENTIS SI PEDE OR.

CAMOMILE

(Chamaemelum nobile)

THIS HERBE IS CALLED CAMOMYL, THE VERTUY OF this herbe is thus, if it be doike w wine it will breke the stone and distroyeth the yelow evel. It helpeth y akying and the disease of y lyver, if it be strained it helpeth and swageth y lozes in a mans mouth, it is good for aking in a mans head, and for the megri, this herbe is hoote and drye.

ANTHONY ASKHAM, *A LITTLE HERBALL*, 1550

GREATER CELANDINE

(Chelidonium majus)

Take vinegar, white wine, the juice of celandine, and plantain, mix them together in a pan, cover over and let them stand therein three days and three nights, take it hence, keep it in a box and anoint thine eye therewith.

The Physicians of Myddfai, 13th century

herbe Centauria maior.

huius genera sunt duo
. has autem centaurias
duas chironcentaurus di
citur inuenisse. inde et
nomine ipsius centau
ri nomen eis imposure.
Ipse nero, de his herbes
herbis medicapa instru
it. prunisq; egritu
tibus tradidre.

CENTAURY

(Erythraea centaurium)

Take the centaury, boil well in old ale, then remove the herbs from the ale, and pound well in a mortar, boil again well, and express through a fine cloth, take this juice mixed with twice the quantity of honey, boil moderately and habituate yourself to take it fasting for nine days, and through the help of God it will heal the oppression and pain about the heart.

THE PHYSICIANS OF MYDDFAI, 13th century

Of centaury: 'If it be joyned with the bloude of a female lapwing or black plover and be put with oyle in a lampe, all they that compasse it aboute shal beleve themselves to be witches so that one shall beleve of an other that his head is in heaven and his fete in the earth. And if the aforesaid thynge be put in the fire whan the starres shine it shall appeare y' the sterres runne one agaynste another and fyght.'

THE SECRETS OF ALBERTUS MAGNUS, Anon

A PAGAN ROMAN PRAYER TO THE EARTH GODDESS

HEAR, I BESEECH THEE, AND BE FAVOURABLE TO MY prayer. Whatsoever herb thy power dost produce, give, I pray, with goodwill to all nations to save them and grant me this my medicine. Come to me with thy powers, and howsoever I may use them may they have good success and to whomsoever I may give them. Whatever thou dost grant it may prosper. To thee all things return. Those who rightly receive these herbs from me, do thou make them whole. Goddess, I beseech thee; I pray thee as a suppliant that by thy majesty thou grant this to me.

Now I make intercession to you all ye powers and herbs and to your majesty, ye whom Earth parent of all hath produced and given as a medicine of health to all nations and hath put majesty upon you, be, I pray you, the greatest help to the human race.

From a 12th century herbal

29

FENNEL

(Foeniculum vulgare)

AGAINST MENTAL VACANCY AND AGAINST FOLLY; PUT into ale bishopwort, lupins, betony, the southern *or Italian* fennel, nepte, water agrimony, cockle, marche, then let the *man* drink. For idiotcy and folly, put into ale, cassia, and lupins, bishopwort, alexanders, githrife, fieldmore, and holy water; then let him drink.

LEECH BOOK OF BALD, BOOK 1, Chapter LXVI, 10th century

THE FENNEL IS WARM AND DRY IN THE SECOND DEGREE and is useful for diseases of the eye. It is good for every kind of poison in a man's body, being drank in the form of powder mixed with white wine or strong old mead. It is useful for tertian ague and inflammatory fever; and if the seed of herb is boiled in water, till it is strong of the virtues of the herb, and the head, when subject to the headache, washed therewith, it will greatly benefit and cure the same, when the headache is occasioned by cold or fever. It will remove the headache very quickly.

THE PHYSICIANS OF MYDDFAI, 13th century

Femenhin.

Nature. c. cr-s. in. r. melior ex eo. romestie. Juuamenti.
ası er filuestri. nocumentis. flitui mesenioz. remotio
noci. cp noceis er hamle.

Alea.

G. nature. c. in. & .fi. z°. melius er eo. modice acuitatis.
Juuamentum. tossicis. nocumentum. expulsine a cerebro.
remotio nocumenti. cum acetoso et oleo.

GARLIC

(Allium sativum)

Take a clove of garlic, prick in three or four places in the middle, dip in honey and insert in the ear, covering it with some block wool. Let the patient sleep on the other side every night leaving the clove in the ear for seven or eight nights unchanged. It will prevent the running of the nose and restore the hearing.

The Physicians of Myddfai, 13th century

HOREHOUND

(Marrubium vulgare)

Take the white horehound, and pound well, then add some pure water thereto, letting it stand for three hours, then strain through a fine cloth, add a good deal of honey to the strained liquor, and put on a slow fire to warm; take half a draught thereof every three hours, and let your diet be the best wheaten bread and milk; when thirsty, take an apple, and cover it with good old cider, eat the apple, in an hour drink the cider, and let this be your only diet.

THE PHYSICIANS OF MYDDFAI, 13th century

1. FOR COLDS IN THE HEAD, AND IN CASE A MAN HREAKS heavily *(makes great efforts to clear his throat of phlegm)*, take this wort, which the Greeks name πράσιον, and the Romans marrubium, and also the English call it horehound, seethe it in water, give to drink to them that hreak heavily; it will heal *them* wonderfully.
2. For sore of maw *(stomach)*, take juice of this same wort, give *(the sufferer)* to drink; it doth away the sore of the

34

maw; and if fever vex him, give him this same wort in water to drink freely, it will raise him up.

3. For tape worms about the navel, take this same wort marrubium, and wormwood, and lupins, of all these worts alike much by weight, seethe in sweetened water and with wine, twice or thrice, lay to the navel; it killeth the worms.

4. For sore of joints and for inflation, take this same wort, burn it to ashes, apply it to the sore, soon it healeth.

5. For swallowing of poison, take ooze of this same wort, give (*to the sufferer*) to drink in old wine, soon the poison passes off.

6. Against scab and against tetter, take this same wort, seethe it in water, wash the body therewith, where the sore may be; it removes the scurf and the tetter.

7. For lungs disease, take this same wort, seethe it in honey, give it to swallow; he will be wonderfully healed.

8. For all stiffnesses of the body, take the same wort, pound it with lard, lay it to the sore; it healeth wonderfully.

THE HERBARIUM OF APULEIUS, 11th century

MANDRAKE

(Atropa mandragora)

1. THIS WORT, WHICH IS NAMED *ΜΑΝΔΡΑΓΌΡΑ* , IS MICKLE and illustrious of aspect, and it is beneficial. Thou shalt in this manner take it, when thou comest to it, then thou understandest it by this, that it shineth at night altogether like a lamp. When first thou seest its head, then inscribe thou it instantly with iron, lest it fly from thee; its virtue is so mickle and so famous, that it will immediately flee from an unclean man, when he cometh to it; hence, as we before said, do thou inscribe it with iron, and so shalt thou delve about it, as that thou touch it not with the iron, but thou shalt earnestly with an ivory staff delve the earth. And when thou seest its hands and its feet, then tie thou it up. Then take the other end and tie it to a dogs neck, so that the hound be hungry; next cast meat before him, so that he may not reach it, except he jerk up the wort with him. Of this wort it is said, that it hath so mickle might, that what thing soever tuggeth it up, that it shall soon in the same manner be deceived. Therefore, as soon as thou see that it be jerked up, and have possession of it, take it immediately in hand, and twist it, and wring the ooze out of its leaves into a glass

Ature c̄ iȝ̊. ſ. ī 2̊. Meliuſ ex ea groſſum ex
ea Iuuamentum uene ſciatice & coytui & o
dorem aromaticat ori. Nocumentum cordi. Remo
tio nocumenti cum ferculiſ unctuoſiſ.

ampulla, *or pitcher*, and when need come upon thee, that thou shouldst therewith help any man.

2. For head ache, and in case that a man may not sleep, take the ooze, smear the forehead; and the wort also in the same manner relieveth the head ache; and also thou wondrest how quickly the sleep cometh.

3. For gout, though it be very heavy, take of the right hand of this wort, and *also* of the left, of either hand by three pennies weight, reduce to dust; give to drink in wine for seven days, *the patient* will be healed not only so that *the remedy* allayeth the swelling, but also leadeth to healing the tugging of the sinews, and wonderfully healeth both the disorders.

THE HERBARIUM OF APULEIUS, 11th century

OF THE SEVEN HERBES THAT HAVE GREAT VERTUE . . .

MARIGOLD

THE FIRST HERBE IS CALLED WITH THE MEN OF Chaldia, Elos, with the Greekes, Matuchiol, with the the Latines, Elitropium, with the Englishmen, Marigold: whose interpretation is of Elion, that is the Sun, and Tropos, that is alteration, or chang because it is turned according to the Sun. The vertue of this herbe is merveilous: for if it bee gathered, the Sunne being in the signe Leo in August, and wrapped in the leafe of a Lawrell, or Bay Tree, and a Wolfes tooth added thereto: no man shall be able to have one word to speake against the bearer thereof, but words of peace: if any thyng bee stolne, if the bearer of the things before named, lay them under his head in the night, he shall see the Theefe, and all his conditions. Moreover if the aforesaide herbe bee put in any Church, where women be, which have broken matrimony on their part: they shall never be able to go forth of the Church except it be put away. And this last point hath been proved, and is very true.

THE SECRETS OF ALBERTUS MAGNUS, Anon

MARIGOLD

(Calendula officinalis)

TAKE MARIGOLD, POUND WELL WITH GOOD WINE, vinegar, strong mead, or strong ale. Strain carefully, and drink a good draught in the morning fasting, whilst the pestilence lasts. If you are taken ill, you will need no other than this as your only drink. It is a good preservative against the foreign pestilence called the plague.

THE PHYSICIANS OF MYDDFAI, 13th century

bis. Oremus. Oratio.

Omine iesu xpe fili dei
viui pone passionem cruce
et mortem tuam inter iudiciũ
tuam et animã mea nunc et in
hora mortis mee et semper lar
giri digneris viuis miaz et gra
ciam deffunctis requiem et ve
niã ecclesie tue pacem et verã
concordia et nobis pctoribus vi
tam et leticiam sempiternã.
Qui viuis et regnas deus. Per
omnia secula seculorum. Ame

Benedicamus
domino.
Deo
gra
ti
as.

WILD MARJORAM

(Origanum vulgare)

1. FOR SORE OF THE HEAD, TAKE JUICE OF THIS WORT WHICH is named serpyllum, and by another name ὀρείγανον, and oil, and burnt salt, bruise it to very small dust, mix all together, smear the head therewith; it shall be whole.

2. Again, for the head ache, take this same wort serpyllum, sodden, pound it in vinegar, smear therewith the temples and the forehead.

3. If one be badly burnt, take this same wort serpyllum, and ashthroat, *or vervain*, one bundle, and by weight of one ounce of the filings of silver, *or litharge*, and roses by weight of three ounces, then pound all together in a mortar, then add thereto wax and of grease of bear and of hart, by weight of half a pound, seethe all together; purify it, and lay it to the burn.

THE HERBARIUM OF APULEIUS, 11th century

Nature c . & f . 7 3 . Melius exca plus aroma
ticans . Iuuamentum confortat stomachum &
cerebrum & omnia uiscera & apit oppilationes i
cerebri . Nocumentum nullum nisi nimis utatur .

IN THE MONASTERY GARDEN

AMONGST MY HERBS SAGE HOLDS THE PLACE OF honour; of good scent it is and full of virtue for many ills. Then there is rue, with its blue-green leaves and short-stemmed flowers, so placed that the sun and air can reach all its parts. Great is its power over evil odours. Southernwood of the hair-like leaves cures fever and wounds; it has well nigh as many virtues as leaves.

Next wormwood, what can equal this for fever and gout. For headache use an infusion of it and plaster your head with a crown of the wet leaves. Horehound is bitter to the palate yet its scent is sweet. Drink horehound hot from the fire if you are poisoned by your stepmother. Fennel deserves high praise, both for its taste and smell. It is good for weak eyes.

WALAFRID STRABO, *THE LITTLE GARDEN (HORTULUS)*, 9th century

MUGWORT

(Artemisia vulgaris)
FOR HYSTERIA

Take mugwort, red fennel and red mint, boil well in old ale, and strain carefully through a cloth; drink it warm and you will recover.

THE PHYSICIANS OF MYDDFAI, 13th century

NETTLE

(Urtica Dioica)

Take the juice of this herb mixed with white wine, strain carefully, and let it cool. Drink some thereof night and morning; it will cure you of the jaundice, renovate the blood, and remove any disease existing therein. If the juice is taken, mixed half with barley wort, it will cure the pleurisy of the side, and will renovate and invigorate an aged man in body and mind.

THE PHYSICIANS OF MYDDFAI, 13th century

Petrosilium.

Natu.... c.... ?.f. in.2. melius ex co? est semen eius. iuuame͠
tum. prouocat urinam. et aperit opilationes. nocumentum.
 diaheu remotio nocume͠ et p͠ouocantibus siturem.

PARSLEY

(Petroselinum crispum)

THE PARSLEY IS A GOOD HERB OF A WARM HOT NATURE, and moist in the third degree. It is useful in all foods as a generator of blood. It will remove obstructions of the veins and arteries in a man's body, so that the humours may circulate properly as they should. This it will certainly do. It is well to employ parsley for the relief of fainting, tertian ague, pleurisy and dropsy, the juice being taken for three days successively without any other drink. It will stimulate the spirits greatly, and strengthen the stomach.

THE PHYSICIANS OF MYDDFAI, 13th century

ROSEMARY

(Rosmarinus officinalis)

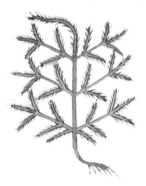

TAKE THE FLOWERS, MIX WITH HONEY, AND EAT THEM daily fasting. You will not suffer from nausea or other noxious condition. It will remove the colic for three hours. Take also the leaves of rosemary and woodsage; making them into a potion and adding honey. It is an excellent remedy for the stranguary, stone and catarrh.

Also, put their flowers or leaves under your head in bed, and you will not be troubled with disagreeable dreams, or oppressed with anxiety of the mind. Also if you carry a stick or fragment of this shrub, no evil spirit can come near you, or any one do you any harm.

It is useful as a lotion for the head when affected with a headache from cold or fever, or when a man is threatened with insanity.

By washing each morning with the decoction and allowing it to dry naturally, the aged will retain a youthful look as long as they live. Should a man have debilitated himself with venery, he will be restored to his usual strength, if he confines himself to this as his only drink for nine days.

It will also cure impotence, in either sex, if used with food. When a couple are childless, let the wife, if young, use rosemary.

THE PHYSICIANS OF MYDDFAI, 13th century

TAKE THE FLOWERS THEREOF AND BOYLE THEM IN fayre water and drinke that water for it is much worthe against all manner of evils in the body.

Take the flowers thereof and make powder thereof and binde it to thy right arme in a linnen cloath and it shall make thee lighte and merrie.

Take the flowers and put them in thy chest among thy clothes or among thy Bookes and Mothes shall not destroy them.

Boyle the leaves in white wine and washe thy face therewith and thy browes and thou shalt have a faire face.

Also put the leaves under the bedde and thou shalt be delivered of all evill dreames.

Smell it oft and it shall keep thee youngly.

BANCKE'S HERBALL, 1525

ROSES

Melrosette is made thus. Take faire purified honye and new read rooses, the whyte endes of them clypped awaye, thā chop theym smal and put thē into the Hony and boyl thē menely together; to know when it is boyled ynoughe, ye shal know it by the swete odour and the colour read. Fyve yeares he may be kept in his vertue; by the Roses he hath vertue of comfortinge and by the hony he hath vertu of clensinge.

Syrope of Rooses is made thus. Some do take roses dyght as it is sayd and boyle them in water and in the water strayned thei put suger and make a sirope thereof; and some do make it better, for they put roses in a vessell, hauing a strayght mouthe, and they put to the roses hote water and thei let it stande a day and a night and of that water, putting to it suger, thei do make sirope, and some doe put more of Roses in the forsaid vessel and more of hote water, and let it stande as is beforesaide, and so they make a read water and make the rose syrope. And some do stāpe new Roses and then strayne out the joyce of it and suger therwyth, they make sirope: and this is the best making of sirope. In Wynter and in Somer it maye be geuen competently to feble sicke melācoly and colorike people.

Sugar Roset is made thus – Take newe gathered roses and stāpe them righte smal with sugar, thā put in a glasse XXX. dayes, let it stande in ye sunne and stirre it wel, and medle it well together so it may be kept three yeares in his vertue. The quātitie of sugar and roses should be thus. In IIII. pound of sugar a pounde of roses.

Oyle of roses is made thus. Some boyle roses in oyle and kepe it, some do fyll a glasse with roses and oyle and they boyle it in a caudron full of water and this oyle is good. Some stampe fresh roses with oyle and they put it in a vessel of glasse and set it in the sūne IIII. dias and this oyle is good.

Rose water. Some put rose water in a glass and they put roses with their dew therto and they make it to boile in water thā thei set it in the sune tyll it be readde and this water is beste.

ANTHONY ASKHAM, A LITTLE HERBALL, 1550

GATHERING HERBS

Plants should be gathered 'at the moment of their full maturity and their greatest vigour'.

For a certain number of plants this time naturally falls in summer, and, because the hours of the solstice have from time immemorial been considered particularly propitious, tradition has it that plants should be gathered on St. John's Day, or Midsummer Day. This is why so many different herbs and plants have come to be called 'St John's wort'.

Now, according to meteorological conditions, geographical situation, aspect and altitude, the ideal moment will vary from year to year. The determining factor should therefore be observation of the plant itself and not mere observance of tradition.

It is best to gather plants on a dry and sunny day. You should not start to pick them too early in the day, nor continue too late, on account of the dew – damp flowers and leaves deteriorate rapidly and so almost completely lose their virtues.

Jean Palaiseul, *Grandmother's Secrets*, 1972

Ruta.

Natura. c. 1. s. in. 3. melior ex ea. orta prope ficum. auiam
tum. acuit uisum. et uentositatem dissoluit. nocumentu
excitat sperma 1 reuerit testiculum coytus. remotio nocumti.
cu multiplicantibz sperma.

RUE

(Ruta graveolens)

1. IF BLOOD FLOW FROM THE NOSE, TAKE THIS WORT, which is named ruta, and by another name like that, rue; apply it frequently to the nostrils; it wonderfully stanches the blood from the nostrils.

2. For bloatedness, take this same wort rue, give it so green, in pieces, to be eaten or swallowed in drink.

3. For sore of the maw, take seed of this same wort and sulphur and vinegar; administer *(to the patient)* to eat, fasting.

4. For sore of eyes and swelling, take this same wort rue, well pounded, lay it to the sore, also the root pounded, and smear therewith; it well amendeth the sore.

5. For the disease which is called lethargy, and in our language is denominated forgetfulness *or unconsciousness*, take this same wort rue, washed, *that is, macerated* in vinegar, souse then the forehead therewith.

6. For dimness of eyes, take leaves of this same wort, give them *(to the sufferer)* to eat fasting, and give *(them him)* to drink in wine.

7. For head ache, take this same wort, give it to be drunk in wine; again pound the same wort, and wring *(out)* the ooze into vinegar; then smear the head therewith. This wort also is beneficial for carbuncles.

THE HERBARIUM OF APULEIUS, 11th century

SAGE

(Salvia officinalis)

THEY ARE USEFUL WHEN BOILED TO STRENGTHEN THE nerves. If an infusion sweetened with honey is drank, it is useful for the lungs. If the foetus in utero is dead, let the woman boil sage with white wine, strain it carefully, and she will be delivered of the same with safety to her life. Also pound this herb, apply to a poisoned wound, and it will extract the poison; though the wound be full of corruption, it will be cleansed to the very bottom. It is a good thing for those in health to drink half a draught in the morning fasting of this potion, in order to preserve health.

THE PHYSICIANS OF MYDDFAI, 13th century

1. FOR ITCHING OF THE SHAPES, *OR THE VERENDA*, TAKE THIS wort, which is named salvia, *or sage*, seethe it in water, and with the water smear the shapes.
2. Again, for itching of the settle, *or seat*, take this same wort salvia, seethe it in water, bathe the settle; it will relieve the itching in a high degree.

THE HERBARIUM OF APULEIUS, 11th century

Salina.

Nature. c. q. h. i. z̊. melior ereca. domestica. Iuuamentum
paralesi. et neruis. nocumentum. denigrat capilos. remotio
nocumen. cum lesiuys in quo sir mire.̊ et ciui orientalis.

SOUTHERNWOOD

(Artemisia abrotanum)

To cure one who talks in his sleep

Take southernwood, and pound it well, and add thereto some wine or old mead, strain well, and let the patient drink a portion thereof night and morning.

The Physicians of Myddfai, 13th century

DRYING AND STORING

To DRY PLANTS WELL, YOU NEED A CONSTANT temperature, good circulation of air, dryness and shade. In the Middle Ages, glassless windows would have ensured these conditions.

1. Always dry plants in a place that is easily ventilated, and in the shade, as the sun's heat can destroy volatile principles such as the essential oils of aromatic herbs. Never dry in bright light as this can discolour or bleach the flowers.

2. As soon as you return from gathering your plants, spread them out: if left in a bag or basket they will rot.

3. There is no need to wash the plants before drying them as they must only be gathered in areas free of any pollution.

4. Never put one plant on top of another for fear of damp or mildew.

5. Plants can be hung from hooks in a dust free room or dried flat. If the latter, they must be turned for the first few days.

6. Once plants are completely dry, cut or crumble the harvest of leaves, stems or flower tips, ready for use or storage. Store in airtight glass or stone containers in a dark place, or better still, in terracotta pots: this will keep them fresh. No light or damp should be allowed to impair the contents.

VERVAIN

(Verbena officinalis)

TO PREVENT DREAMS

TAKE THE VERVAIN, AND HANG ABOUT THE MAN'S NECK, or give him the juice on going to bed, and it will prevent his dreaming.

THE VIRTUES OF VERVAIN

THE WHOLE PLANT IS GOOD FOR ALL DISEASES proceeding from the poison of scrophula, whether affecting the lungs, liver, kidneys, brain, eyes, or any part. Gather this, and any other herb in the name of God, and give no heed to those who say that it should be gathered in the name of the devil.

THE PHYSICIANS OF MYDDFAI, 13th century

VIOLET

(Viola odorata)

THE VIOLET IS CALLED IN GREEKE, *ION*: IN LATINE, *Nigra viola* or blacke Violet, of the blackish purple colour of the floures. The Apothecaries keepe the Latine name *Viola*, but they call it *Herba Violaria*, and *Mater Violarum*: in Spanish, *Violeta*: in English, Violet. *Nicander* beleeveth that the Grecians did call it *Ion*, because certain Nymphs of Iönia gave that floure first to *Jupiter*. Others say it was called because when *Jupiter* had turned the yong damosell *Iö*, whom he tenderly loved, into a Cow, the earth brought forth this floure for her food; which being made for her sake, received the name from her: and thereupon it is thought that the Latines also called it *Viola*, as though they should say *Vitula*, by blotting out the letter *t*.

The floures are good for all inflammations, especially of the sides and lungs; they take away the hoarsenesse of the chest, the ruggednesse of the winde-pipe and jawes, and take away thirst.

There is likewise made of Violets and sugar certaine plates called Sugar violet, Violet tables, or Plate, which is most pleasant and wholesome, especially it comforteth the heart and the other inward parts.

John Gerard, *The Herball or Generall Historie of Plantes*, 1597

WORMWOOD

(Artemisia absinthium)

1. This wort, which is named absinthium, and by another name ware-moth, or *wormwood*, is produced in cultivated places, and on downs, and in stony places.
2. In order that a man may remove from the body weals and other sores, take this wort absinthium, seethe it in water, then put it on a cloth, lay it to the sore; if then the body be tender, seethe it in honey; lay it to the sore.

The Herbarium of Apuleius, 11th century

YARROW

(Achillea millefolium)

1. Of this wort, which is named millefolium, and in our language yarrow, it is said that Achilles, the chieftain, should find *(found)* it; and he with this same wort healed them who with iron were stricken and wounded. Also for that reason, it is named of some men, Achillea. With this wort it is said that he also should heal *(healed)* a man whose name was Telephos.

2. For tooth ache, take a root of this wort, which we named millefoil, give it *(to the patient)* to eat fasting.

3. For wounds which are made with iron, take this same wort, pounded with grease; lay it to the wounds; it purgeth and healeth the wounds.

4. For a swelling, take this same wort millefoil, pounded into butter; lay it to the swelling.

5. In case that any man with difficulty can pass water, take ooze of this same wort with vinegar, give it him to drink; wondrously it healeth.

6. If a wound on a man be chilled, take then the same wort millefoil, and rub it very small, and mingle it with butter, lay it then on the wound; soon it quickeneth and warmeth it.

7. If a mans head burst, or a strange swelling appear on it, let him take roots of this same wort, and bind them on his neck; that will come to be of good service to him.

8. Again for the same, take this same wort, work it to a dust; apply it to the wound, then it will soon be heating.

9. If any mans veins be hardened, or his meat will not digest, take juice of this same wort, then mingle wine and water and honey and the juice all together, then give it him warm to drink; then it will soon be well with him.

10. Again, for ache of the bowels and of all the inwards, take this same wort, dry it then, and rub it to dust, very small; then put up five spoons full of the dust, and three cups of good wine; then give him that to drink. Then it is good for him for whatsoever annoyances he hath within.

11. If then, after that, there befall the man hiccuping, or any ratten-burn within (him), take then roots of this wort, pound them very well; put them into good beer; give it him then lukewarm to sup. Then I ween that it may be of good benefit to him either for hiccup or for any internal difficulty.

THE HERBARIUM OF APULEIUS, 11th century

IN A PLEASURE GARDEN

BEHIND THE LAWN THERE MAY BE GREAT DIVERSITY OF medicinal and scented herbs, not only to delight the sense of smell by their perfume but to refresh the sight with the variety of their flowers, and to cause admiration at their many forms in those who look at them. Let rue be set in many places among them, for the beauty of its green foliage and also that its biting quality may drive away noxious vermin from the garden. There should not be any trees in the middle of the lawn, but rather let its surface delight in the open air, for the air itself is then more health-giving. If the [midst of the] lawn were to have trees planted on it, spider's webs stretched from branch to branch would interrupt and entangle the faces of the passers-by.

If possible a clear fountain of water in a stone basin should be in the midst, for its purity gives much pleasure. Let the garden stand open to the North and East, since those winds bring health and cleanliness; to the opposite winds of the South and West it should be closed, on account of their turbulence bringing dirt and disease; for although the North wind may delay the fruit, yet it maintains the spirit and protects health. It is then delight rather than fruit that is looked for in the pleasure garden.

THE SECRETS OF ALBERTUS MAGNUS, Anon

Acknowledgements

Grateful thanks to Mary Shadbolt for advice on herb lore, past and present.

Text acknowledgements:
Barrie & Jenkins Ltd for permission to reprint extracts from *Grandmother's Secrets* by Jean Palaiseul (1972)

Picture credits:

Biblioteca Casanatense, Rome 13: *Tacuinum Sanitatis f. LXVIII*

Bibliothèque Nationale, Paris Cover, 5: *MS NA Lat 1673 f. 32*, 4: *MS NA Lat 1673 f. 34*, 31: *MS NA Lat 1673 f. 41*, 32: *MS NA Lat 1673 f. 25*, 46: *MS NA Lat 1673 f. 31*, 54: *MS NA Lat 1673 f. 32*, 56: *MS NA Lat 1673 f. 343*

Bodleian Library, Oxford 21: *MS Douce 310, Book VII*, 23: *MS Bodley 130 f. 26*, 24: *MS Bodley 130 f. 44*, 25: *MS Ashmole 1462 f. 31v*, 26: *MS Ashmole 1462 f. 23*, 35: *MS Ashmole 1462 f. 26*, 38: *MS Ashmole 1462 f. 45*, 48: *MS Ashmole 1462 f. 33*, 58: *MS Douce 310, Book XXIV*, 64, *MS Ashmole 1462 f. 35v*

Bridgeman Art Library/Bibliothèque Nationale, Paris 19: *MS 12322 f. 188*, 61: *MS FR 913661*

Bridgeman Art Library/British Library 41: *Add MS 35214 f. 49b-50*, 52: *MS Roy 14 E VI f. 157*, 62: *Add MS 35214 f. 49b-50*

British Library, London 7: *Add MS 34294 f. 110 v*, 50: *MS Harl 4425 f. 184b*

Giraudon/Bibliothèque Municipale, Laon 29

Giraudon/Bibliothèque Municipale, Rouen 37, 43

Scala/Biblioteca Estense, Modena 67: *MS Lat 209 DX2 14 c. 10r*